What Would Jane Do?

What Would Jane Do?

THE WIT AND WISDOM OF JANE AUSTEN

SUZIE GROGAN

To Peter, my very own Mr Knightley.

Illustrations by Luna Willems.
Portrait of Dr. Buchan in Public Domain.
All other images courtesy of Shutterstock.

This edition published in 2025 by Arcturus Publishing Limited
26/27 Bickels Yard, 151–153 Bermondsey Street,
London SE1 3HA

AD012445UK

Printed in China

Contents

For those who want to know every detail of their favourite author's life, Jane Austen's biography is frustratingly short. She didn't keep a diary, or at least not one that is known about, and of the many letters she exchanged, mostly with her sister Cassandra, only 160 survive. None of those were written until her twentieth year. At least one biographer has pointed out that her brother's brief biographical sketch of her, for the posthumous publication of *Northanger Abbey* and *Persuasion,* is not entirely accurate. 'Short and easy will be the task of the mere biographer... A life of usefulness, literature and religion was not by any means a life of event,' he says. The extent to which any of her novels were autobiographical is not known. The lives of those around her were not free from scandal, and her relationships with brothers, sister and friends were interesting, but it is unlikely that sibling rivalry, domestic disharmony and romantic liaisons formed most of her experience.

Her brother seemed intent on avoiding any comparisons between the characters in her novels and those in her circle: 'Her power of inventing characters seems to have been intuitive, and almost unlimited. She drew from nature; but, whatever may have been surmised to the contrary, never from individuals.' And yet even he admits that the voice in her letters is the same as that in her books. Perhaps his motive in protesting at her inspiration was to avoid her readers spectulating on which family members inspired which characters, and thereby opening up certain members to ridicule.

Her wisdom and wit shines through in both fiction and correspondence. As such, it is easy to extract quotations from her works that have resonance for us today. There is a universality to the experiences she describes that continue to provide not just entertainment but sage advice for how to conduct oneself in society and in relationships. It is this wise counsel that we find in her works – whether spoken by favoured characters or in reaction to the foolish ones. The words of a wide range of the cast from her books can be found on the cards included with this book. You can pick a card a week throughout the year and display it upon the stand provided so that you can enjoy having Jane right there with you upon your desk in daily life.

Jane Austen was born in the tiny Hampshire village of Steventon on the 16th of December in the freezing winter of 1775. Her father was the Reverend George Austen and her mother, his wife Cassandra. Six children had been born before her, all boys apart from her beloved sister, also Cassandra, born in 1773.

Steventon was a remote village, housing fewer than thirty families, who lived off the land growing turnips, or beans. Sheep were kept for meat and wool, spun by the women of the parish, and George Austen, as Rector, collected tithes directly from the farmers, tying his income to theirs. The rectory, as the grandest house, was the last in the village and it was her home well into adulthood. As a family, the Austens were comfortable rather than well-off, but both parents were well-educated, and family connections gave them opportunities to mix with wealthier families nearby. The soil around the village was said not to be good, and with the inhabitants poor, and poorly educated, so this society was much needed.

Steventon Rectory was Jane Austen's home for the first 25 years of her life. Situated then in a valley surrounded by fields, it is no longer standing, having been demolished shortly after Jane's death. In 1870, James Edward Austen-Leigh, her nephew, described it as a "sufficiently commodious" house. As the Revd. Austen took in pupils to add to the family income, it would need to be sizeable, eventually housing parents, the seven children of the family, servants, and pupils.

Mrs Austen, unlike some other mothers of her class, believed in breast feeding her babies, but after a few months the children would be weaned and fostered out to a local 'dry nurse' until their mother was happy that they could walk and talk and act sensibly. This was strange even to contemporary views, but the parents apparently visited each day, and the children returned home at about two years of age. It worked well, as all the children survived and flourished into adulthood, even Jane's disabled elder brother George.

Even a larger house might have been too cramped to sleep them all comfortably, which may partly explain why Jane and Cassandra were sent away to school so young. Jane was just seven and by the time they returned to the house, in 1786 or 87, she would have attended schools in Oxford, Southampton (where she nearly died of typhus) and Reading, where from 1785 to 86 the sisters went to the Abbey House School. Their education included lessons in writing, spelling, French, history, geography, needlework, drawing, music, and dancing. Separation at such a young age, and the loss of freedom school brought about, left her with a dislike of girls' schools that she took into adulthood, and her relationship with her mother has sometimes been described as 'cool'.

Private schooling at home amongst the Revd. Austen's extensive book collection, to which the family appeared to have free access, likely seemed more useful and interesting. The library is said to have housed over 500 books, and Jane particularly enjoyed history, writing her own humorous version of Goldsmith's *History of England*, which still survives, illustrated by her sister. They, too, participated in the lessons enjoyed by their brothers and the pupils, while Mrs. Austen later reminisced about the family routine of two daily lessons in Virgil, despite the exclusion of female family members from learning Latin or Greek. Jane's older brothers consistently organized theatrical performances, a family tradition that persisted for numerous years, and visits and gifts from her cousin Eliza, who happened to be married to a French Count, brought a welcome exoticism to her intellectual life.

We know little of what Jane borrowed from her father's library, but it is well known that all the family read novels which, in the late 18th century, remained a fresh form. Many of the works would be considered 'low-brow' popular fiction, which were gobbled up, particularly by Jane and her father, as avidly as Henry Fielding. Immersing herself in the daily lives of fictional characters – both admirable and flawed – served as the ideal learning opportunity for a prospective novelist. By the time she turned eighteen, she had already written several early pieces, and at nineteen, she wrote *Lady Susan* on a desk purchased for her by her father. By the age of twenty-two, she had drafted the initial versions of *Sense and Sensibility* and *Pride and Prejudice*, titled *Elinor and Marianne* and *First Impressions*, respectively.

However, she was fully aware of her unpreparedness for any profession and disliked the idea of teaching, anyway. Even in adulthood, until her books started selling well, she had little money of her own apart from a small allowance from her father, so her future was not her own to decide. By the mid-1790s, two of her brothers had joined the clergy, two others became Admirals in the Royal Navy and one, Edward, was adopted by Mr and Mrs Thomas Knight and inherited their wealthy estate in Kent. Despite having had brief love affairs, Jane and Cassandra remained unmarried.

THE MEANS TO MARRY

The girls lacked a dowry. The Revd. Austen lacked the necessary financial stability or prudence to save money for his daughters. In about 1794, Cassandra became engaged to Thomas Fowle, who went abroad to earn the money to marry, contracted yellow fever and died, leaving his fiancée with £1,000, which at least gave her a little security.

Jane exuded charm and wit, earning the admiration of men. In 1795, she crossed paths with Irishman Tom Lefroy, the nephew of her friends, which allowed her to embrace her first romantic infatuation. Attending balls and parties, they spent a lot of time together, giving Jane something to share with her sister. There has been speculation about why this romance came to nothing, but there is nothing in her letters to suggest an acrimonious split. Lefroy returned to Ireland, where he eventually married and in time became the country's most senior judge.

LIFE IN BATH

The period at her beloved Steventon was ending by the turn of the century. In 1800 the Revd Austen was 70, with a wife often in poor health. His son, James, was ready to take over the living. In 1801 the Revd George Austen retired, and he and his wife, with Jane and Cassandra, left Steventon and settled in Bath. The transition proved to be sudden and challenging, despite visits back to see James and his family, and upbeat letters to Cassandra, listing the compensations of Wales and the sea over an increasingly monotonous Basingstoke social life.

Bath didn't agree with Jane, and her literary output dwindled. The Austens rented number 4 Sydney Place from 1801 to 1804, and whilst there they went on holidays to popular seaside resorts in

the West Country. A visit to Lyme Regis, in Dorset, with its cobbled streets, gardens and the Cobb, a broad harbour wall popular for a stroll then, as now, inspired her to set scenes in a later book, *Persuasion*, in the town.

During this period, to the surprise of many of her readers today, Jane Austen received a marriage proposal. At the beginning of December in 1802, Jane and Cassandra were staying with friends near their old home at Steventon. Harris Bigg-Wither was an old friend from childhood. He was heir to Manydown Park and, although apparently shy, with a stutter, would have made Jane a very secure marriage. She was six years older than him at the time – he was just twenty-one – and although she initially accepted him, she quickly realised that this young man, who had very little interest in books and was certainly not much like an Austen hero, would not do. After accepting him (she must have liked him, and being the mistress of an estate was, after all, tempting for a woman who wanted to marry) the idea of greater intimacy with him made marriage impossible. She changed her mind, told Harris the next morning, and fled back to Bath with Cassandra as quickly as she could. Perhaps that proved to be the only time she felt glad to be back.

When the lease on Sydney Place expired, the family moved to number 3 Green Park Buildings East, where Mr Austen died on 21st January 1805.

The sudden passing of her father, following a short illness, proved to be a substantial loss to Jane, who had always cherished his unwavering support for her writing career. She wrote to her brother Frank on 21st

January: “We have lost an excellent Father. An illness of only eight and forty hours carried him off yesterday morning between ten and eleven. His tenderness as a father, who can do justice to?” The burial of George Austen took place at St Swithin’s Church, the same location where he had wed Cassandra, Jane’s mother, more than forty years prior.

Jane, her mother and sister, with no pension bequeathed to them, were left with very little money. Mr Austen had left everything to his wife, but his income from tithes and a small annuity just stopped and no provision had been made for his daughters. Their combined income was now around £210 per year, including interest on the money left to Cassandra by Thomas Fowle. The lease agreement for Green Park Buildings was upheld for the next three months, but, unable to prolong it, the women moved to 25 Gay Street, Bath, a smaller house where they required only one maid. They were joined by Martha Lloyd, an old family friend who lodged with them. Although it isn’t possible to visit the house in Gay Street, the Jane Austen Centre is just a few doors down and offers a reconstructed version of the author’s life in Bath.

A PLACE TO WRITE

But her life underwent another upheaval, and she spent her early thirties living a nomadic lifestyle, the three women staying briefly with, or in close proximity to, family and attempting to settle down in Southampton, near Jane's brother Francis and his family. By this time, she knew that her chances of marrying and having her own home were dwindling, and she had to be content with visits to Godmersham or her old home at Steventon to help with her nephews and nieces. None of the women found a new circle of friends, so when Edward, the wealthiest member of the family, offered them a cottage close to Godmersham, they accepted and at last found a home to settle in, and a place Jane felt she could write.

> *Our Chawton home — how much we find Already in it, to our mind, And how convinced that when complete, It will all other Houses beat*
>
> *Jane Austen, in a letter to her brother Frank, 26th July, 1809*

In July 1809, aged 33, Jane moved, with her mother and sister, to a house on the Chawton estate, inherited by her elder brother Edward from wealthy relations. The 'Chawton House' visited by Jane Austen's admirers from all over the world is what she referred to in her letters as 'The Great House', whilst they occupied what has become known since as the 'Cottage', a home first built in the 1500s but much improved, in the village about 400m away. Both homes are open to the public.

To make it suitable for the ladies, a significant amount of work had to be done on the cottage, but what had once been a farmer's house turned out to be quite comfortable. The family entered through a door directly on the road, which bustled with stagecoach traffic, generating more noise and dirt than a visitor encounters today. The house was double fronted, offering rooms to the right and left. These the household used as a dining and drawing room. The house contained six bedrooms and a garret for the servants. There was a garden big enough to walk in for exercise, surrounded by a high fence for privacy.

Her friend and companion, Martha Lloyd, went with them and the all-female household made a happy team, practising domestic economy and stretching their limited income by making their own clothes, wine and beer.

Jane played the piano and enjoyed walks into the Hampshire countryside with her companions, and she wrote whilst her sister and Martha managed the house and her mother concentrated on the lovely cottage garden that surrounded them. Chawton provided her with the opportunity to write the majority of her well-known novels and dedicate time to revising *Elinor and Marianne* (*Sense and Sensibility*), which was accepted for publication in 1810.

In the darker evenings, there would be parlour games, and those needing a little skill, like spillikins (where the object was to pick up the most sticks), or reading aloud to one another from favourite authors such as George Crabbe and William Cowper. Visitors would see the furniture pushed back to allow a space for dancing. They did not have a wide circle in the village, but saw old friends from Steventon and socialised with Frank and his family.

Those darker evenings would be long as winter set in at a time when Jane Austen would have little light to write by. Many years passed before gas lamps in homes became commonplace, and candles emitted little light. High-quality beeswax candles carried a hefty price tag, while the cheaper alternatives, such as tallow or rushlights, emitted unpleasant smells and smoke. Families would enjoy the light and heat from the fire, despite the numerous terrible stories about the inflammable nature of Georgian clothing that appeared in the press as the cause of women's deaths.

The life at Chawton suited her so well that it is there that she built confidence as an author. For the first time since she moved from her childhood home at Steventon, Jane felt able to devote her time to writing. There was more space than in Bath, and she didn't seem to miss the opportunities for socialising that the city had offered. She could walk in the gardens of her own home and at the Great House at Chawton and enjoy fresh air and peace.

In 1810 she was glad of her brother Henry's help in finding a publisher for *Sense and Sensibility*, Thomas Egerton, who also published *Pride and Prejudice* three years later. When *Mansfield Park* and *Emma* were ready for publication, she shrewdly kept the copyright to both books and funded the publication herself, the former through Egerton and *Emma* through the fashionable publisher John Murray, who also published works by Byron, Goethe and Charles Darwin. Although cutting about the Prince Regent in private, she agreed to dedicate *Emma* to him. He did not respond.

By 1815, despite her growing fame and the comfort of her life at Chawton, Jane found herself increasingly unwell. Her writing matured, and in that year she began *The Elliots* (later published as *Persuasion*) but in the following year, 1816, writing became increasingly difficult. Henry helped her regain control of *Lady Susan*, (published as *Northanger Abbey*) but neither book would be published before her death.

Before her death, she gathered her strength and began what readers know as her last novel, but before the spring arrived, she had managed just twelve chapters before her health forced her to abandon the project. She called this novel '*The Brothers*', but today it is '*Sanditon*', often reimagined and completed by others.

Jane's illness, whatever it may have been, seemed too severe for local doctors to handle (in reality, for any doctor of the time to handle). Jane and Cassandra moved to lodgings in College Street, Winchester, fifteen miles from Chawton. Arriving on 24th May, 1817, Jane and Cassandra found their cramped lodgings close to the Cathedral in Winchester. Dr Lyford, a respected surgeon at the County Hospital in the town, attended her regularly, but her condition worsened. Less than two months later, on 18th July, 1817, she passed away and was laid to rest in Winchester Cathedral on the 24th. She was just 41 years old.

Her will reads:

"I Jane Austen of the Parish of Chawton do by this my last Will & Testament give and bequeath to my dearest Sister Cassandra Elizth everything of which I may die possessed, or which may be hereafter due to me, subject to the payment of my Funeral Expences, & to a Legacy of £50. to my Brother Henry, & £50. to Mde Bigeon [Henry's cook] – which I request may be paid as soon as convenient. And I appoint my said dear Sister the Executrix of this my last Will & Testament." 27th April, 1817.

Identifying Jane

For many years, those with an interest in Jane Austen have longed to know what she looked like, but even after examining what is available in forensic detail, there is no definitive answer.

So, as we follow Jane through Georgian and Regency England, what image of her should we rely on?

Well, work on her size and shape is now generally accepted. Clothing known to belong to Jane has been analysed and expert Hilary Davidson calculates she stood between 5ft 6 and 5ft 8 inches tall. When the average height for a man in the period was just 5ft 6, it is obvious she would be viewed as a tall woman, and with measurements around bust, waist and hips at a maximum of 33 inches, 24 inches, and 34 inches, a very slender one. Mary Russell Mitford, a neighbour, said, uncharitably, that she could be compared to a poker – 'perpendicular, precise, taciturn.'

Her face is much more mysterious. Her image has adorned British currency for many years, but the plump image, based on what was said at the time to be an unflattering portrait by her sister Cassandra, has been challenged in recent years by other representations. The only other officially recognised painting of Jane, also by Cassandra, obscures the author's face and a silhouette that is 'possibly' of Jane Austen (found in an early copy of Mansfield Park) gives us little more information.

In recent years, however, Austen scholar Paula Byrne, author of *The Real Jane Austen: A Life in Small Things*, received a drawing her husband bought at auction, thinking it resembled Jane, and on the back discovered her name, misspelled. Two experts have since accepted this as a portrait painted in about 1815, because in it she strongly resembles her brothers, with a piercing gaze and the confidence of a woman who has enjoyed success as a writer. It is not sentimentalised or sweetened by illustrators over time, as Cassandra's portrait has been.

Although some suggest that Jane Austen's style of dress verged on dowdiness, author Hilary Davidson meticulously researched the letters to discover that Jane was well aware of and interested in changing fashions. She was keen to adapt and repurpose existing outfits but also alive to anything new that could enhance the wardrobes of herself and her sister Cassandra. When the family moved to Bath in 1801, and into 4 Sydney Street, she made ordering a dress from the local seamstress, Mrs Mussel, a priority.

Perhaps the descriptions that we should accept most readily are those of people who knew her well. Based on the account by her niece Caroline, she had a face that was more round than long, in addition to a bright, clear brown complexion instead of a pink one. Her eyes were hazel and 'She was not… an absolute beauty, but… a very pretty girl. … Her hair, a darkish brown, curled naturally.' Another niece, Anna said, after praising many of her features, 'One hardly understands how with all these advantages she could yet fail of being a decidedly handsome woman.' She had a face 'lively and full of humour' remarked a family friend. By the time she died, her hair, whilst still curly, was flecked with grey.

More recently, the Jane Austen Centre in Bath commissioned a full-length waxwork figure of Jane, sculpted by Mark Richards. The figure was dressed in authentic-period costume by Bafta and Emmy award-winning designer Andrea Galer; it shows a modest, attractive woman and looking at it, it is possible to see the determined woman who completed six of the most sharply observed and best loved novels in the English language.

Jane Austen spent her life surrounded by family and friends. We know little about her day-to-day life as a child, but from later letters and biography we can assume that apart from general family squabbles among siblings, and with parents, she lived in a close-knit and affectionate circle. Remarkably for the period, her mother, Cassandra Leigh Austen, had eight children and all survived into adulthood, even a brother who was born with significant disabilities.

Reverand George Austen, born 1731, died 1805.
People described George Austen, Jane's father, as a handsome man, tall, slim, and good looking, with wavy brown hair and 'bright hazel eyes'. An

intelligent man, he studied at St John's College, Oxford, where he gained a reputation known as 'the handsome Proctor.' He had a love of literature and his duties as Rector of Steventon did not prevent him from enjoying life as a small-time gentleman farmer. He also took in pupils whose lessons his children could sometimes join in. Works on the parsonage redeveloped it over time and eventually he could keep a coach. His position in society, and that of his wife (who came from aristocratic stock) was enough to secure the respectability and social life of an upper middle class family.

Cassandra Austen, nee Leigh, born 1739, died 1827 (10 years after Jane.)

Cassandra Austen, Jane's mother, was the daughter of Revd. Thomas Leigh and his wife, Jane. She possessed wit, chattiness, and an excellent sense of humour. At the age of six, she had already started writing entertaining verses. In spite of facing health issues throughout most of her married life, she proved to be proficient as a housekeeper, needlewoman, and gardener. She had to part with several front teeth when her children were young, which had an impact on her appearance, but she always took pride in her fine 'aristocratic' nose.

James Austen, born 1765, died 1819

Jane's eldest brother, James, gained recognition as the poet within the family and during his studies at Oxford University, he took on the role of editing a periodical named 'The Loiterer'. He followed his father into the clergy, taking over the living at Steventon after George Austen retired. Jane didn't get on with him well: 'his time here is spent I think in walking about about the House & banging the Doors'. In spite of his fondness for animals, he had an enthusiasm for hunting, although he occasionally experienced mild melancholia and dealt with health problems from his forties onward. Like Jane, he died relatively young.

George Austen, born 1766, died 1838

George junior is the mystery in the Austen family. Not much is known of his life, and none of it was spent with Jane. A cognitive impairment or learning disability was present from birth, leading to him being boarded away from the family home and Jane having no contact with him. He lived to old age.

Edward Austen, later Knight, born 1767, died 1852

Edward was a popular man, full of fun, and a good businessperson. Distant cousin Thomas Knight and his wife Cassandra were childless, and looking for an heir when they formed an attachment to the third son of the Austens, Edward, who would be formally adopted by them. When he inherited the estates in Kent and Hampshire in 1812, he changed his name to Knight. He was the first to marry, but his wife Elizabeth died, aged just 35, having their eleventh child. Biographers suggest Edward's income and capital made him richer than Fitzwilliam Darcy.

Henry Austen, born 1771, died 1850

Henry Austen, despite being an Oxford scholar like his elder brother, possessed a much livelier personality, brimming with charm and optimism, and shared his father's captivating hazel eyes. He is said to be Jane's favourite brother: 'most affectionate and kind', she wrote. Henry was tall with his father's bright hazel eyes and possessed of an irrepressible optimism. He served as a militiaman, and established himself as an army agent and banker, before failing in business and becoming the second Austen sibling to enter the church.

Cassandra Austen, born 1773, died 1845

When Jane was born, her father saw her as a playmate for little Cassy, and indeed Jane and Cassandra were best friends all their lives. Cassandra never married; her fiancé, the Reverend Tom Fowle, went to the

West Indies to earn money for the wedding, where he contracted and died of yellow fever in 1797. Affectionate and focused on family, Cassandra frequently visited her brothers and assisted with their many children. She and Jane would read novels aloud, tend the garden and bees and write to each other endlessly when apart. Jane called her 'the finest comic writer of the present age'. She offered her wholehearted support to Jane, managing the home to give her opportunities to write. Sadly for biographers, she burned many of Jane's letters to her after her sister's death.

Francis (Frank) Austen, born 1774, died 1865

Frank Austen was an interesting child, described as 'friendly' and 'unruly' with a mop of curly, dark hair. An enterprising boy, he hunted from a young age and at just twelve, went to the Royal Naval College in Portsmouth, experiencing the many brutalities of life at sea at the height of the Napoleonic Wars despite a short stature and slight frame. He was a religious man, and a gentleman, but was ruthlessly correct and efficient and a strict disciplinarian. With ambition driving him, he achieved the rank of Admiral of the Fleet and received a knighthood in 1837.

Charles Austen, born 1779, died 1852

Much the youngest of the siblings, born five years after Frank, Charles also went to Naval College and became known as a sweet-tempered, handsome, charming and popular chap, who, though less ambitious than his elder brother, obtained high rank through good nature. His letters home were shared around to much enjoyment and he would always return home with presents for everyone. His sisters consistently referred to him as 'our own special little brother' and they always eagerly awaited communication from their brothers at sea, hearing about their lives, promotions and fellow sailors.

An honorary sister – Martha Lloyd, born 1765, died 1843

'With what true sympathy our feelings are shared by Martha you need not be told; she is the friend and sister under every circumstance.' *Jane to Cassandra, 13th October, 1808*

Ten years older than Jane Austen, Martha Lloyd became a lifelong friend. Meeting as young people, as neighbours at Steventon, they formed an immediate bond that, despite separations, lasted until Jane Austen's death. When the Revd Austen died, Martha, having recently lost her mother, joined Mrs Austen,

Jane and Cassandra to form a comfortable household, moving with them to Southampton and Chawton. Martha and Cassandra combined their skills to ensure Jane did not need to let domestic duties prevent her writing. The women would shop together, attend balls and stay up late talking about their deepest secrets.

Martha had been left scarred by a smallpox epidemic that killed her brother. Smallpox was a highly contagious disease and killed up to 60 per cent of those contracting it, maiming and blinding many survivors. Inoculation against it, which Edward Jenner developed, became available in the late 18th century, but epidemics continued to claim lives well into Victorian times.

After Jane Austen died in 1817, Martha remained with the family, acting as housekeeper, and in 1828 married Jane's then widowed brother Frank. Then 62, she eventually became Lady Austen, enjoying 15 years of a late marriage. She stayed close to Cassandra into old age.

Jane Austen cast a keen eye across the society and times she lived in and provided us with a fascinating insight into everyday life in the Georgian era. Here we look more closely at the themes in her books and how they relate to the realities of life at the time.

FROM ROUT CAKES TO RAGOUT OF BEEF

Fans have always been interested in what Jane Austen, and her family, ate and we are lucky in that both her sister Cassandra and their great friend and housemate from late in their residency in Bath, Martha Lloyd, kept excellent records. Jane too, responsible as she often was for the housekeeping, mentions food in her letters, and of course in her books.

To a 21st-century reader, it is not what Georgians ate, but when they ate it that comes as the greatest surprise. The main meal of the day, during Jane's childhood in the 1780s, for instance, was consumed between 3pm and 5pm. Lunch was a relatively new idea, and eating early added supper to the menu as something to eat when peckish before bedtime.

Breakfast

When Jane took on the responsibility of breakfast as an adult, she would serve it at around 9am, toasting bread or muffins and serving them with butter, alongside pound cake. Tea would start the day off well, but occasionally she exchanged it for cocoa. More affluent families might make eggs or meats available, take coffee and tea and breakfast as late as 10am. However, it was common to have taken some exercise before breakfast, such as strolling in the neighbourhood, as Ann does in *Persuasion*, or 'seeing to the horses' as Edward Ferrars does, awkwardly, in *Sense and Sensibility*. Jane Austen describes shopping before breakfast as if it were commonplace.

Earlier in the Georgian period, the full breakfast of meat and eggs, accompanied by ale, would be eaten early in the day to fortify working men who would have little but a snack until their dinner, but by Jane's time this was dying out. Poorer families had to survive on a penny loaf, porridge or gruel (boiled oats), drinking 'small beer' brewed with a lower alcohol content and safer than drinking water. Often men would have been at work for two hours before they stopped for bread and butter and tea.

Luncheon

It was only during the later Regency period that lunch gained popularity, in part due to the shift towards later dinners and the need for something to quell hunger around the middle of the day. Visits to friends and social acquaintances took place at any time between breakfast and dinner, and those hosting would provide light refreshments. Elizabeth Bennet visits Miss Darcy at Pemberley and is served 'cold meat, cake and a variety of the finest fruits'.

We would recognise the sandwiches, cake and fruit on the menu today. By the end of the period, it was already middle and upper class 'ladies who lunched' in the main.

Dinner

Dinner was a more filling and, for the richest, lavish affair. Providing it, and eating it, held significance as a matter of class in Georgian England. Families ate earlier in the country than in town, and the lower classes earlier than the richest, as Jane Austen subtly points out in *Pride and Prejudice*. For example, walking to the Bingleys to see Jane, Elizabeth walks in on the family breakfasting when she has eaten much earlier. In the same book, the Bennets eat dinner earlier than the Netherfield family does.

The choice of food depended on where the family lived and the accessibility of ingredients. 'Locally sourced produce' meant exactly that. The Austen family grew a lot of their own food and preserved it for consumption in the winter. They raised their own animals for the table and could afford to eat well. Dishes would include mutton, beef or a chicken dish with vegetables. During this period, keeping food fresh was not easy and, once stored, it was often shared with mice, rats, and other pests. In the summer, meat and dairy could be stored anywhere in the house that offered the coolest temperatures, but it spoiled quickly. The household at Chawton regularly preserved food in jars, Martha adding the recipes to her household book. The very wealthy had

'ice-houses' in the garden, dug slightly underground and filled with ice dug from frozen lakes, or bought from whaling vessels. Ice cream and sorbet had already gained popularity as desserts.

The popularity of French cooking grew, and Jane mentions a 'ragout' of veal or beef. In spite of the more glamorous name, this still simply involved stewing or casseroling meat, but it would add variety to their otherwise wholesome and plain English plates. They would have enjoyed sweet desserts, made using dried fruits, and those grown in their garden. They kept a servant, so Mrs Austen, Cassandra and Jane did not have to undertake tasks such as making bread, again a sign that their aspirations were higher than their labouring neighbours, although Jane did help in the kitchen. The presence of ovens was uncommon among poorer families in towns, forcing them to rely on their local baker or pie man if they wanted to have anything other than a soup or stew.

For those at the highest tables, eating the most lavish dishes, table manners could still give away the unwary. Dishes, sweet and savoury, would be brought out en masse, then cleared and further courses offered. One must be careful not to reach for dishes further down the table and be sure to offer a dish to those seated next to you first. In later years, dining at Godmersham with brother Edward and his family, food would be more varied and much richer. White soup was popular, with fish and meat dishes such as a haunch of venison, goose or a ragout of beef. The menu included salmon and mackerel, in addition to seafood options like lobster and oysters, which were readily available at that time and inexpensive for even the poorest to eat. Sweet dishes such as jellies, syllabub or baked custards were Austen favourites and her heroines are never watching their waistlines – eating what they want when they are hungry and walking off any extra calories consumed.

Supper

Where many less well-off families would go to bed when darkness fell, and wake with the light, higher up the social scale a formal ball could continue until dawn and card games could last into the early hours of the morning, so supper became the last meal of the day. In *Emma*, Mr Woodhouse and Emma's sister Mrs John Knightley liked to take a basin of gruel as their supper, although Hartfield could provide more attractive options, such as tarts and custards, as well as wine.

Jane Austen's books, and her letters, are infused with references to food, to produce and to her pleasure in housekeeping and the garden.

"I always take care to provide such things as please my own appetite, which I consider as the chief merit in housekeeping. I have had some ragout veal, and I mean to have some haricot mutton to-morrow."

Mrs Bennet, in *Pride and Prejudice*, uses food competitively, and as a sign of social standing:

"The venison was roasted to a turn – and everybody said they never saw so fat a haunch. The soup was fifty times better than what we had at the

Lucas's last week; and even Mr Darcy acknowledged that the partridges were remarkably well done; and I suppose he has two or three French cooks at least."

In *Emma*, food is used by Mrs Elton is a similar way, but for Emma herself, despite the need for social niceties, there is warmth and fellow feeling:

"Father, not everyone shares your dislike for rich foods. You may eat your gruel, but we shall dine on roast chicken, ragout veal, potatoes, biscuits, vegetables, and apple dumplings."

Good food must be praised, but gluttony is not. As Emma says to her father, "I am certain that if we have ailments when we are advanced in years, we shall remember all your cautionary advice on what we should have or should not have eaten in our youth." The Revd. Dr Grant of Mansfield Park is not a main character, but an example of what becomes the unpleasant over-eater: '...when Dr Grant had brought on apoplexy and death, by three great institutional dinners in one week'.

By this period, it was becoming 'unladylike' to enjoy one's food and eat heartily, as women did in her early works. Anne Elliot and Elizabeth Bennet are apparently unbothered by the necessity to eat – Elizabeth preferring the plain dishes of her childhood to the then popular French style – and Jane Fairfax and Marianne Dashwood have poor appetites that, at times, concern their friends. Women could be plump and jolly, but grossness is reserved for men.

Martha Lloyd, the family friend who stayed with them for many years, particularly at Chawton Cottage (eventually marrying Jane's brother Francis) kept a 'Household Book' for many years, detailing recipes, remedies and domestic hints and tips to aid in the smooth running of a home. That book, the original of which is held in the Jane Austen House museum at Chawton, offers a glimpse of what the Austen women liked to eat.

The orchard offered up greengages and plums, currants and gooseberries which Martha might work with their cook to preserve, or use for gooseberry cheese, or currant wine.

Toasted cheese was one of Jane's favourites (it is even mentioned in *Mansfield Park*) and is included with recipes for mead, made with honey from their own bees, which Jane was fond of and would ask after in her letters, Baked Apple Pudding and Apple Snow and the rather plainer Hogs pudding, like a black pudding without the blood, containing pork fat and oats.

From a picnic to a lavish dinner, Jane Austen's books are filled with the joy of food. Here is the recipe for 'rout cakes', specifically mentioned in *Emma*. They are a little like rock cakes and not difficult to make.

'To make rout drop-cakes, mix two pounds of flour with one pound of butter, one pound of sugar, and one pound of currants, cleaned and dried. Moisten it into a stiff paste with two eggs, a large spoonful of orange-flower water, as much rose water, sweet wine and brandy. Drop the paste on a tin plate floured, and a short time will bake them.'

Mary Eaton, *The Cook and Housekeeper's Dictionary*, 1822

FASHION IN REGENCY ENGLAND

In 1811, a 'Lady of Distinction' published *The Mirror of Graces*, which advised young women of the appropriate way to dress. Consider the Bennet girls in *Pride and Prejudice* getting ready to go to the ball as the Lady describes:

'In the spring of youth, when all is lovely and gay, then, as the soft green, sparkling in freshness, bedecks the earth; so, light and transparent robes, of tender colours, should adorn the limbs of the young beauty... Her summer evening dress may be of a gossamer texture; but it must still preserve the same simplicity, though its gracefully-diverging folds may fall like the mantle of Juno... In this dress, her arms, and part of her neck and bosom may be unveiled: but only part. The eye of maternal decorum should draw the virgin zone to the limit where modesty would bid it rest.'

The same rules do not apply to an older woman, such as Mrs Bennet:

"As the lovely of my sex advance towards the vale of years, I counsel them to assume a graver habit and a less vivacious air...At this period she lays aside the flowers of youth, and arrays herself in the majesty of sobriety, or in the grandeur of simple magnificence... Long is the reign of this commanding epoch of a woman's age; for from thirty to fifty she may most respectably maintain her station on this throne of matron excellence."

It is not clear what is expected post menopause, which reflects both the life expectancy and social expectations of older adults of the time.

Jane Austen's period of publication sits within the strict definition of 'Regency', that is the period 1811 to 1820, but her work on the books started much earlier than that, during what has been referred to by historian Hilary Davidson as the 'long regency' period from 1795 to 1825, which covers some interesting changes in the way men and women presented themselves, and covers a period when English fashion became obsessed with neo-classicism (the art and fashions of Ancient Greece and Rome) and with Renaissance detailing. Men's fashion had a more military bearing, and was more practical than previous 17th and 18th century outfits.

A gentleman would dress in a manner suitable for both town and country. Breeches composed of wool, linen, or the more luxurious silk material were fastened at the knee with ties or buckles and featured a front flap for convenience. Buckskin versions offered a snugger fit, but all were held up by braces. 'Beau' Brummell later made slightly longer breeches fashionable. Stockings were usually wool or cotton, or silk stockings requiring frequent mending. Riding boots became popular – leather to the knee as worn by the military. White shirts, waistcoats and long jackets would be fitted for gentlemen by their tailor, but the poor had to make do with whatever was affordable and to hand patch with materials such as sacking. Families made their own clothes, bought second-hand garments and adapted ill-fitting clothes and shoes to make do. Working men and women often wore clogs.

We are used to seeing Jane Austen adaptations where young women are wearing high-waisted white or pastel coloured muslin dresses, and indeed that material had just then started being imported from Asia at prices that became within the reach of the upper middle classes. What we consider 'typical' of the period is a dress with a high waist, wide neckline and long sleeves, perhaps covered, when cool, with a short spencer jacket and worn with a bonnet. A suntan was for the labourer. The undergarments consisted of a linen shift (similar to nightwear) and stays, or a corset. These were boned and laced at the back, worn to maintain a good figure.

In the Victoria and Albert Museum in London, there is a dress worn by seventeen-year-old Mary Dalton Norcliffe, dated 1807. It is a simple sash-tied white muslin dress, developed unfussily from the dresses Mary would have worn from the nursery into her teens. Later she would have progressed into stiff bodied gowns and seems, in fact, the embodiment of the fashionable woman described by a 'Lady of Distinction'.

However, there were more practical requirements of dress – white muslin and pumps would have been no use to Jane on her extended walks around Steventon or indeed the muddy, horse-dung-covered streets of

Bath. 'Pattens' had a wooden sole and were worn as an overshoe for outside wear. Stout boots were available, alongside more elegant ones. In *Emma*, the heroine wears a laced 'half-boot'.

As the period went on, Georgian men dispensed with powdered wigs, preferring to wear their hair natural. For women, a cap was seemly. Jane Austen made many and wore her hair washed, brushed and tucked under one to save trouble.

Historians have frequently proposed that Jane herself did not have an interest in clothes, and she barely mentions them in her books. However, these books were written over a period, and fashions changed. To write in detail of something that might need a lot of revision, especially when it wasn't even certain when the books would be published, is as risky now as it was in the past. Jane Austen's books have been so popular for such a long time it is possible for readers to think of them as historical fiction, but she wrote for her contemporaries, who would have known what was 'in'. It is also easy to suggest from Jane's letters that she wasn't interested in what she wore, or even cared. One writer suggests that should she be alive today, she would be most comfortable in an old tweed skirt and cardigan. But that is not the Jane who wrote to her sister in 1814:

'I wear my gauze gown to-day, long sleeves and all. I shall see how they succeed, but as yet I have no reason to suppose long sleeves are allowable. I have lowered the bosom, especially at the corners, and plaited black satin ribbon round the top. Such will be my costume of vine-leaves and paste...Mrs Tilson had long sleeves, too, and she assured me that they are worn in the evening by many. I was glad to hear this.'

Not much clothing belonging to Jane survives. All we know of is a pelisse (a long coat, opening at the front and high-waisted like the fashionable dresses worn underneath) a shawl, a topaz cross, and a turquoise ring and bracelet. Mrs Austen, Cassandra and Jane displayed a keen interest in needlework, creating and repurposing their clothing, but that doesn't imply that she disregarded her appearance. The family had their social position to maintain. In fact, Hilary Davidson gives Jane's budget for 1807, which shows that her income for the year was fifty pounds, fifteen shillings and sixpence (£50 15s. 6d.), and of that thirteen pounds, nineteen shillings and threepence (£13 19s. 3d.) was spent on "Cloathes & Pocket," a quarter of it.

If you are interested in the world of fashion in Jane Austen's lifetime and in her books, there is one expert who has worked harder than many to establish the reality of Jane Austen's wardrobe. *Dress in the Age of Jane Austen: Regency Fashion*, by Hilary Davidson, is a wonderful source book and highly recommended.

SOCIAL CLASS IN GEORGIAN ENGLAND

Jane Austen lived through a period when not only did women have very little power or voice in society, but when the vast majority of the population was excluded from influence on any political decisions – even ones that affected them directly. The power was in the hands of those who owned the most land, or the most money – the aristocracy, or those who made their fortunes in trade or banking and could buy themselves into the corridors of power.

In 1814, during Jane Austen's 38th year, Patrick Colquhoun published his 'Treatise on the Wealth, Power, and Resources of the British Empire' and outlined a structure of English society that emphasises the significance of social class during Jane Austen's lifetime and suggests why it is frequently satirised in her novels.

The highest class included: The Royal Family, Archbishops of Canterbury and of York, the Bishops of London, Durham and Winchester, certain other bishops of the Church of England, Life Peers, the Earl Marshal, Lord Great Chamberlain, hereditary peers and 'all above the degree of a Baronet, with their families'. (In 1814 there were up to 3,000 people in this category.)

The second class included Baronets, Knights, 'Country Gentlemen', and 'others having large incomes' (unspecified) with their families (up to 250,000 of these) and the third class included 'Dignified Clergy', the top Statesmen, Lawyers and Physicians, 'considerable Merchants' and large-scale manufacturing families. This still lofty assembly also contained 'bankers of the first order'. Colquhoun estimated there were fewer than 100,000 in this class in 1814, but the numbers would soar as the century progressed.

After this, the fourth, fifth, and sixth classes contained characters that rarely feature in Jane Austen's novels. A somewhat arbitrary 'fourth class' bracketed the 'lesser and respectable clergy', 'state employees', 'Persons holding inferior situations in Church and State', 'respectable Clergymen of different persuasions' (not defined), 'Practitioners in Law and Physic' (presumably surgeons, apothecaries and other medics not considered third class), 'Teachers of Youth of the superior order', 'respectable Freeholders', 'Ship Owners', 'Warehousemen and respectable Shopkeepers', 'Artists', 'respectable Builders, Mechanics, and Persons living on moderate incomes, with their families'. According to Colquhoun's estimation, the number of people in this category, including their families, was less than 1.5 million. Even as we get down to 'fifth class', including some shopkeepers, innkeepers, publicans and 'persons engaged in miscellaneous occupations or living on moderate incomes', we haven't met the bulk of the English populace.

It is in the sixth class that most of us live. 'Working Mechanics, Artisans, Handicrafts, Agricultural Labourers, and others who subsist by labour in various employments, with their families' form well over 60 per cent of the population in the Georgian period. Colquhoun estimates nearly 8,800,000 artisans and labourers living in what would then be decent but subsistent conditions.

The armed forces – that is, the Army and Navy – were a separate category of their own. In *Persuasion*, Jane Austen examines the changes in social structure that allowed a self-made Navy man to raise his social standing to where marrying into the gentry was acceptable.

The very lowest, or seventh, class includes 'Paupers and their families', 'Vagrants, Gipsies, Rogues', 'Vagabonds', and 'idle and disorderly persons, supported by criminal delinquency'. In this period, there are nearly two million families living hand-to-mouth in this way.

Reading Jane Austen is to immerse oneself in a world where crime seemed non-existent, yet she lived during a period that was marked by the notorious 'Bloody Code', an era when the adage 'You might as well be hung for a sheep as a lamb' held true in its literal sense. The death penalty applied to stealing either, so those who could not otherwise feed their family, or who rustled sheep for profit, might as well 'go big'. During Jane Austen's lifetime, the lawmakers raised the number of capital crimes, punishable by hanging, to over 200. Some of these would now just result in a caution. The gap between rich and poor was widening, and inevitably, those in this lowest class were the ones caught and punished – the son of a landowner could buy his way out of trouble because many of the laws were there to protect his father's property.

Jane Austen lived through a period of revolution – the French Revolution of 1789 and the Napoleonic Wars, lasting from 1803 to 1815 – so this social and political unrest form a backdrop to her life. By the time she died, the middle classes to which her family belonged were becoming more involved in public life. Not until the Victorian period did the middle class and their interests start to impact political decisions.

Income and class

Jane Austen writes, quite openly, of the incomes of her characters, placing them nicely within these social boundaries. At the time the novels were written, money invested in government funds offered 5 per cent a year on larger fortunes and 4 per cent on smaller investments. Mr Darcy is said to have an income of £10,000 a year. The fortune realising that income is £200,000. All who know of him are aware he is a very wealthy man. By comparison, Mr Bennet, with five daughters and a wife to support, has an income of £2,000 a year, the same as the bachelor Colonel Brandon in *Sense and Sensibility*. The Bennet family is relatively comfortable, but in order to survive respectably, their daughters must make good marriages.

Caroline Bingley, also in *Pride and Prejudice,* is an example of a woman of fortune. Her £20,000 pounds would give her an income of £1000 per year. This makes her both independently wealthy and a very good marriage prospect.

A poor curate such as Edward Ferrars in *Sense and Sensibility* would earn about £100 a year, a low income that would give the lady of the house only a maid of all work to help her. Colonel Brandon considers £300 enough for a single man, but insufficient to support a family. Therefore, the Revd. George Austen and his wife Cassandra (Jane's parents) would have been struggling financially with just £200 to support their whole family at Steventon.

Mr Elton in *Emma*, Mr Collins in *Pride and Prejudice*, Edward Ferrars in *Sense and Sensibility*, Edmund Bertrum in *Mansfield Park* and Henry Tilney in *Northanger Abbey* are all members of the clergy, enjoying very different positions in society and taking more or less interest in their flock. Jane Austen utilises members of the clergy – particularly Mr Elton and Mr Collins – to emphasize flaws in a profession where genuine religious conviction was not necessary. Mr Collins is obsequious and oily, and Henry Tilney, regularly holidaying in Bath, seems hardly aware of pastoral responsibilities and is an independently wealthy young man, as many members of the clergy were. It was a career deemed acceptable to the younger sons of wealthier families, especially the wealthier livings on offer, which paid up to £1,000 per year.

A character with two or three servants was offered around £500 in income by Jane Austen. It is what Mrs Dashwood, in *Sense and Sensibility*, has to give Elinor and Marianne a comfortable life. It would not be enough to provide a carriage, however: £1,000 per year makes that comfortable.

Henry Crawford in *Mansfield Park* and Bingley and Darcy in *Pride and Prejudice* all enjoy incomes over £4,000 a year, which is about the level where money can be spent without too much caution. Darcy has, we are told, £10,000 a year to maintain Pemberley.

After the death of her father, Jane Austen, her sister Cassandra and their mother were at the mercy of their male relatives for any support they needed financially. But they lived in *relative* poverty. A small farmer, or a labourer on an estate, might have a maximum of £20 per year to maintain a house and family and a servant, much less. At Chawton, there were two maids, a cook, and a manservant. The importance of managing the household's finances was acknowledged, but they were not poor. In fact, some note that in all her novels, Jane Austen does not describe a character who is so poor they cannot have *any* servants. Jane Austen's is a privileged world. The living conditions experienced by a majority of the population were plagued by poverty. They did not enjoy any education and their favourite pastimes are abhorrent to us two hundred years on – dog and cock fighting and pugilism were bloody and mired in crime. Those scenes are left to Dickens and the Victorians to describe.

ILLNESS AND DEATH IN THE GEORGIAN PERIOD

Jane Austen lived through an exciting period in the history of medicine, although for most people any advances that took place in the Georgian and Regency period would be hardly noticeable. By the time she died in 1817, anaesthetics and antibiotics had not yet been developed, leaving only primitive medicines crafted from long-standing botanical remedies, and an insufficient number of physicians to serve the demands of a constantly increasing populace.

At this time, the majority of medics were apothecaries, with many having already transitioned away from their original role as shopkeepers, supplying herbs and mixtures as requested by the more esteemed physicians. The training of the physician was centred around the university, with minimal involvement in the practical care of patients and was commonly pursued by the younger sons of the aristocracy. The services they provided came at a high

cost and were not as practical as those offered by the apothecary, who, during the early 19th century, frequently underwent training for up to seven years. The apothecary-surgeon served as the cornerstone of the increasing number of teaching hospitals and was relied upon in rural areas, such as Steventon, to treat a range of ailments, from the common cold to cancer, and the traumatic incidents associated with farming and carting accidents.

Beginning in approximately 1810, the Romantic poet John Keats pursued a career as a surgeon-apothecary, and his researchers have acquired significant insights into the everyday experiences of surgeons and patients during this era. Thomas

Hammond, the apothecary to whom Keats was apprenticed dealt with 'fractures, dislocations, gunshot wounds, intestinal obstructions, tapeworms, burns and scalds, difficult births, congenital malformations, tumours, convulsions, gout, accidents, diseases, hernias and so on…' (Nicholas Roe)

As she grew up, Jane must have been aware of the importance of a local medical man – and qualifications were not open to women for decades – because her mother, Cassandra, suffered from poor health all her life. Early in Jane's life, for instance, the loss of many of her front teeth aged her facially and caused disability. In the time preceding the common presence of trained dentists, extraction served as the sole alternative for toothache, and frequently, in rural areas, it was carried out by the doctor or even the blacksmith. If Mrs Austen could afford to travel and pay for a dentist, there was no anaesthetic and an incompetent dentist might remove gum and bone with the offending tooth. In 1813, Jane took her nieces up to see Mr Spence, a dentist in London, and they still endured a miserable hour or two, undergoing tooth fillings and extractions. 'It was a sad business, and cost us many tears.' (Letter to Cassandra, September 1813). It also seemed to her that the dentist was damaging perfectly good teeth, saying 'he must be a Lover of Teeth & Money & Mischeif' (sic).

At Steventon, they relied on the elderly Mr Lyford, whose family name is linked to the Austen family until Jane's death. In a letter we hear Mr Lyford arrives to treat Mrs Austen just as they are sitting down to dinner and he is asked to join them. In Georgian society, the delight of invitations to dine in the best houses always remained reserved for a family physician. Mr Perry, the apothecary in *Emma*, like all of his profession, was tainted by an association with 'trade' and was *not* invited to dine.

Later, in 1808, Jane mentions another Mr Lyford when she is in Southampton with Cassandra and her mother, and he may have been Charles, the brother of the final Lyford – Giles-King Lyford, surgeon at the County hospital who treated her during her final illness in Winchester.

One benefit of the Austens' move to Bath was the availability of medical treatment, particularly for Mrs Austen who could enjoy the warm public baths, including the most fashionable Cross Bath, a natural hot water spring to which you could be taken, already undressed for bathing, in a sedan chair. Jane regularly walked with her Uncle James to the Pump Room to take the waters, passing the many 'Bath chairs' used by invalids that frequented the streets of a town flourishing on the real or imagined sickness of others.

However, all that medicine offered in Bath could not help Jane's father. In mid-January 1805 George Austen felt 'an oppression in the head with fever, violent tremulousness, & the greatest degree of Feebleness'. Dr Bowen, an apothecary who had already achieved some success with Jane's mother, was summoned but he quickly realised there was little he could do and suggested calling in Dr Gibbs of Gay Street. All he could offer was 'Cupping', a form of bloodletting. Extracting a patient's blood as a means of healing was a commonly accepted method, influenced by the ancient belief in the circulation of the four humours throughout the body. The action was taken even when the patient was already weak, and could frequently worsen their condition. Without knowing the cause of Mr Austen's illness – and there was no knowledge then of bacterial infection, or sepsis, which may have been the cause – cupping posed a risk but it seemed to have a positive effect, allowing the patient to pass a comfortable night and get up for breakfast. The hope turned out to be false, however, as another wave of fever overwhelmed him and this time, there was no recovery. George Austen 'drew his last gasp' at twenty past ten that evening.

The frail Mrs Austen bore it as well as she could and outlived not just her husband, but her youngest daughter Jane too.

From going through her books and letters, it is apparent that Miss Austen has no patience for individuals who pretend to be sick and those who seem to derive pleasure from maintaining a state of perpetual illness. She dealt with her mother's chronic ill-health by avoiding as much conflict as possible, knowing that stress and worry only seemed to make her mother worse. In her novels, there is an acknowledgement that whilst physical illness might be unavoidable, a character's emotional reaction to it can make matters better or, as in Marianne Dashwood's case, much worse. As an author, she acknowledges, though, that for some women, poor health, or claims to it, were the only way to have any control over their life, especially within a marriage. For others, frailty provided protection.

'Tell [Mr Bennet] what a dreadful state I am in,— that I am frightened out of my wits; and have such tremblings, such flutterings, all over me, such spasms in my side, and pains in my head, and such beatings at heart, that I can get no rest by night nor by day.'
Mrs Bennet in Pride and Prejudice

Nora Bartlett points out that in *Sense and Sensibility* there are two deaths, a sprained ankle, four fainting fits, five fits of hysterics, a nervous breakdown, a case of questionable anorexia, and a putrid fever, but as Marianne represents 'sensibility', sympathy is asked of the reader rather than laughter.

Self-care and knowledge of traditional herbal remedies played a vital role in the period, as evidenced by Martha Lloyd's cookbook, partly compiled at Chawton, which includes a 'cure' for 'mad dog bite' and a remedy for pain in the side. Emetics (to make you sick) and laxatives (for constipation) were commonly taken for many complaints and it is easy to forget that there was no way of telling whether something minor, such as a cold, was just that, and not incipient pneumonia.

In 1769, just prior to the birth of Jane Austen, William Buchan released his celebrated work, *Domestic Medicine*. It sold over 80,000 copies, nineteen editions were printed, and it was translated into almost every major European language. Buchan became the 'go to' for general medical queries, and the Austen household may have had one. Listed among the general causes of illness were 'diseased parents', night air, sedentary habits, anger, wet feet and abrupt changes of temperature. The causes of fever included injury, 'bad air', violent emotion, irregular bowels and extremes of heat and cold. Cholera was said to be caused by rancid or putrid food, by 'cold fruits' such as cucumbers

and melons, and by passionate fear or rage. It was hardly surprising that many in Jane Austen's time were anxious about their health.

Jane Austen's death in 1817, at 41, has been the subject of much speculation, research and discussion. She was, even for the times, relatively young and from a family that otherwise lived to a good age. Early in 1816, just after her 40th birthday, she began to complain of fatigue and a pain in her back. She put a lot of her discomfort down to the stresses of family life at the time – her brother Henry's financial troubles, her relationship with her nieces and the regular hosting of family and friends – but her more irritable nature and nighttime fevers were becoming obvious to those around her. She would tell them it was 'bile' – meaning black bile, one of the four humours believed to keep the body in balance – or rheumatism and take to lying down after meals, on three chairs lined up rather than take the sofa from her mother. In letters she played down her symptoms and regularly claimed to be feeling much better, which suggests that whatever condition she was suffering from would return in cycles, building to a feverish crisis before offering some brief respite. Illness was boring, and Jane hated to be bored.

A trip to Cheltenham Spa didn't help, and historians now suggest that rather than Addison's disease as first supposed, she could have had Hodgkin's Lymphoma, a blood cancer, or possibly lupus. A letter written in March 1817, in which she once again professed to be feeling better, talks of skin changes, leaving her face disfigured by black and white patches. For a woman whose complexion had been the envy of many in her youth, this must have been distressing.

In January 1817, she determined to start work on a new novel, *The Brothers*, but had to give up two months later after writing just twelve chapters. The unfinished book, which is now known as *Sanditon,* was not published until 1925.

Jane's illness continued to baffle, causing her increasing disability. The local apothecary in Alton struggled to handle her symptoms and more specialised care was suggested. Giles-King Lyford, a surgeon at the well-respected Winchester Hospital, would take responsibility for her care.

Rented lodgings were found where Dr Lyford made frequent visits, but nothing could be done. Only morphine, near the end, could offer comfort. When she died, on 18th July, Dr Lyford wrote that he 'supposed a large blood vessel had given way', suggesting a speedy and merciful death – something he would have said to the families of many patients eager to know their loved one had not suffered. In fact, Jane Austen suffered through the night, in the arms of her sister, until she fell unconscious and died – with words of relief and a request for prayers on her lips. Whatever had killed Jane Austen, it would be many decades before the history of medicine could offer anything more than opiates to ease her pain.

In Chapter 9 of *Emma*, Austen wryly observes, 'Everybody had a degree of gravity and sorrow; tenderness towards the departed, solicitude for the surviving friends; and, in a reasonable time, curiosity to know where she would be buried.' Burial took place swiftly after death, usually within three or four days, as at that time there was little chance of avoiding a swift decomposition of the corpse, especially in summer. Coffins were often kept open so that relatives could say goodbye, but again the appearance of the departed could be distressing very soon after death. Embalming using chemicals became available in the 18th century but wasn't common practice until the 20th.

In Georgian England, if you survived to the age of thirty, you could hope – serious illness aside – to live to fifty and beyond. But infant mortality, in rural and urban areas, was high. As many as 60-70 per cent of babies and young children died before the age of five, and Mrs Austen was right to breastfeed her babies. It is clear from higher mortality rates among wealthy families in London that sending babies to a wet nurse might increase the risk of death.

For Jane Austen, "In the midst of life we are in death" from the service of burial was a truth generally accepted. She may not face us with death often in her books, but when she does, she is speaking from everyday Georgian experience.

It is said, despite her long association with the city and adoption as literary heroine, Jane Austen never liked Bath. In *Northanger Abbey*, she may have put her own thoughts into the character of Isabella Thorpe: "I get so immoderately sick of Bath; your brother and I were agreeing this morning that though it is vastly well to be here for a few weeks, we would not live here for millions." There is little doubt, however, that the city inspired some of her greatest literary moments – both *Northanger Abbey* and *Persuasion* are set there and it is mentioned in all six of her major works. Catherine Morland in *Northanger Abbey* in particular shows how the magic of the city's history and architecture and lively social scene worked its magic on many who lived a country, rather than London, existence.

"Oh! Who Can Ever Be Tired of Bath?" *Catherine Morland, Northanger Abbey*

Jane Austen lived in four houses in Bath, the first in Queens Square where she lived for a month in 1797 and 1799 whilst her brother took the waters. However, it is 4 Sydney Place that claims her longest residence and a bronze plaque as her principal home in the city. Her parents had married in the city in 1764 and when her father retired from his living at the church in Steventon in 1800, the family had three years in Sydney Place until the lease expired.

George and Cassandra Austen moved with daughters Cassandra and Jane to Sydney Place to enjoy fresher air away from Bath City Centre. When you visit the area today, where there are houses and a church, Jane and her family could look over woods and farmlands and see spring water 'cascading' out of the hills. Walking left from the house, Jane could have strolled to the village of Bathwick – now an upmarket part of Bath itself – where a farm sold fresh milk and eggs, and wealthier families who preferred peace and quiet could live away from hustle and bustle and the smell of coal fires.

Now a Grade One listed building, 4 Sydney Place was built in 1794, at the cost of £700 and designed by a young architect, Thomas Baldwin, in the popular Palladian style. Baldwin was a prominent man during the boom in housing in Bath but was not financially scrupulous. The Austens moved into what was a respectable, and up-to-date home, affordable largely because there were fewer than four years on the lease:

'The situation is desirable, the Rent very low and the Landlord is bound by covenant to paint the two first floors this summer…' an advertisement for Sydney Place in 'The Bath Chronicle' 28th May, 1801.

The rooms were large and high ceilinged, which suited the tall Jane, and grand enough to suit the aristocratic relations on her mother's side of the family. Tall and narrow, over four storeys, there were two rooms front and back, typical of the period, and a lot of stairs.

A parlour or dining room occupied the ground floor, serving as a place for the Austens to receive visitors and for the ladies to engage in activities deemed appropriate for women in the early 1800s. This included letter writing and hours of sewing shirts for their brothers in the navy, along with some of their own clothes.

Jane wrote little of her fiction in Bath, apart from a never published novel entitled *The Watsons*, but she might have edited or read aloud from work drafted at

Steventon. On the same floor, there is a smaller room that may have been George Austen's study.

On the first floor was the grandest room, the Drawing Room, decorated sumptuously with plaster relief work and windows taking in the best aspect over the surrounding area. One large room could be divided into two reception rooms, heated from a fireplace that burned coal, rather than the wood used at Steventon. Coal was brought into Bath by donkeys regularly seen in the streets, collapsing under the weight of their loads. The Drawing Room is the room women might use for music, cards or for 'withdrawing' to after dinner, leaving the gentlemen drinking and smoking at the table. *Pride and Prejudice* features the grand drawing rooms at Netherfield, and at Rosings where Elizabeth is subjected to after-dinner 'chat' from Lady Catherine de Burgh "when the ladies returned to the drawing room, there was little to be done but to hear Lady Catherine talk." Perhaps this reflects Jane's view of drawing room entertainment. She found card parties in Bath boring, with no interesting people to talk to and only sedate and 'proper' gaming.

Although the Austen's would have been smaller than the rooms depicted in the novels, there would be paintings on the wall and beautiful draped curtains at the windows.

The three bedrooms occupied by the family were located up more stairs, with Jane and Cassandra sharing one as they always did, and another room for their parents and a guest room. At the very top, the already exhausted servants would clamber up the narrow, twisty staircase to rooms cramped under the eaves, with windows that let in drafts as the weather swirled about the top of the building. Bath was built for show, and no one wanted to see the servants.

The Austens had three servants: a cook, a housemaid and a man for the heavier work. They worked from the basement, dark and damp kitchens and scullery leading to an outside earth toilet and a small garden. Many of the houses we admire in Bath were built quickly and not well, rushed up to take advantage of the property boom. Often the basement was damp and unsanitary, even when the floors above were gracious and well decorated.

Opposite their new house, the Austens could enjoy the delights of the Sydney Gardens, built on the model of London's famous Vauxhall pleasure grounds. There were swings, and bowling greens and a famous labyrinth that was twice the size of that at Hampton Court Palace. Before they moved to the house, Jane had written to Cassandra, 'It would be very pleasant to be near Sydney Gardens; we might go into the labyrinth every day.' (21st January, 1801). To do that did not come cheap, however. The cost of a subscription at the time they moved away from Sydney Place was seven shillings and sixpence for the season, or two and sixpence a month. Visitors could enjoy being seen for a day at the cost of sixpence, and it was a place to promenade and be seen. Jane wrote again: 'I was walking almost all day long; I went to Sydney Gardens soon after one, & did not return till four.' But it was hardly the same as a walk in the Hampshire countryside around Steventon, and not knowing whether she would ever move back to the countryside, it is not surprising that whatever delights Bath could offer, the smoky, polluted streets and primped and managed green spaces could not make up for the loss of those country spaces.

In 1804, when the lease on Sydney Street ended, the move was made to 27 Green Park Buildings, but tragedy struck soon afterwards when Jane's father, the Reverend Austen, died in January 1805. After just a year at more lowly lodgings at 25 Gay Street, which Jane did not like, Mrs Austen moved her family, with some relief on Jane's part, away to Clifton in Bristol and then to Southampton.

‘It will be two years tomorrow since we left Bath for Clifton, with what happy feelings of escape’ (Letter to her sister, Cassandra, 1808.)

The Themes in Her Novels

'Money can only give happiness when there is nothing else to give it'

MARIANNE DASHWOOD, SENSE AND SENSIBILITY

Sense and Sensibility was published in 1811, and is the first novel published by Jane Austen, although instead of her name as the author, the title page shows it was written 'By A Lady'.

It is the story of two sisters, their relationship and their romantic lives. Elinor and Marianne Dashwood are left with little money after the death of their father, and it is expected that they marry to secure the family's financial future. Jane Austen uses her powers of observation, her wit and humour to contrast Elinor's practical response to romance, her need for privacy and discretion and Marianne's romantic approach, her openness and freedom of expression; the 'sense' and 'sensibility' (or emotion) of the title.

It is a classic look at British middle-class society in the Regency era, highlighting the expectations placed on both men and women, the struggle between reason (the practical nature of Elinor) and emotion and the complex nature of courtship and marriage in the period. By the end, both Elinor and Marianne have found a balance between the two, and made happy marriages, but not before Austen has given us some sparkling and interesting characters to move the plot along.

'It is a truth universally acknowledged, that a single man in possession of a good fortune, must be in want of a wife.'

PRIDE AND PREJUDICE

Pride and Prejudice was published in 1813, again anonymously. It was drafted under the title *First Impressions*, but changed before publication, and the new title describes the themes succinctly. It is witty and charming and Jane Austen's favourite.

Despite being a story of how pride in one's own social standing and a prejudice based only on a brief meeting can stand in the way of true love, Austen also looks at the importance of family, social class and gender inequality. Mr and Mrs Bennet have five daughters and their house and wealth stand to be inherited by an odious cousin, the Reverend Collins. It is therefore vital, in their mother's eyes at least, that the girls make good marriages.

Essentially, this is a love story focusing on the two main characters of Fitzwilliam Darcy and Elizabeth Bennet, who initially dislike each other and eventually, after misunderstandings and realisations, come to love each other tenderly and with a full understanding of each other's character. The reader also follows the romance between Elizabeth's sweet-tempered elder sister Jane Bennet and Darcy's friend Charles Bingley, and the happy ending suggests Jane Austen believed that despite the need to marry for security (in Mrs Bennet's view, and Charlotte Lucas's when she accepts Collins) and to save a reputation (as when Lydia Bennet elopes with Wickham), love can happen outside of the potential barriers of class and societal expectation.

'Selfishness must always be forgiven, you know, because there is no hope of a cure.'

MARY CRAWFORD, MANSFIELD PARK

Mansfield Park, published in May 1814, was the first book entirely conceived and written at Chawton. It is a book that deals more seriously than in other books, with issues of social class and morality, of the difference between town and country and the importance of marriage. It is the only book in which Austen mentions the source of a character's wealth, suggesting Sir Thomas Bertram has built his fortune on the ownership of slaves.

Aged ten, Fanny Price, who lives with her parents in an impoverished part of Portsmouth, is sent to live with her wealthy relatives at Mansfield Park, an estate in Northamptonshire. A naturally quiet and shy girl, she grows into a woman still slightly in awe of her family, most notably her Bertram cousins, Tom, Maria and Julia. Only Edmund, another cousin, is kind to her, and she grows to love him. However, she is not his first choice, and the book considers moral dilemmas, the problems of class and the role of women, as well as alluding to the corruption and exploitation of slavery as a source of income. Despite its intelligence

and serious notes, which for some makes it Austen's most satisfying book, and the sparkier characters of neighbours Henry and Mary Crawford, the book does not rise to the heights of wit of previous books. Some readers find Fanny a frustrating heroine, often an observer rather than actor. However, in the second part of the book much hangs on her actions, as a young woman under pressure from powerful men.

'A single woman, with a very narrow income, must be a ridiculous, disagreeable, old maid! the proper sport of boys and girls; but a single woman, of good fortune, is always respectable, and may be as sensible and pleasant as anybody else.'

EMMA TO HARRIET SMITH, EMMA

Emma was first published in December 1815, by 'the author of *Pride and Prejudice*' and as Jane Austen refused to relinquish the copyright to either this book or Mansfield Park, the costs of publication were met by herself. Despite her dislike and criticism of the Prince Regent, she was encouraged to dedicate it to him. He didn't respond.

At the time of publication, readers were surprised by the lack of 'action', as the story takes place in the fictional rural village of Highbury and the drawing rooms of the characters. However, since then it's themes of marriage, social class and gender have encouraged some reviewers to think it Austen's masterpiece. It is a high comedy, centring on the story of 'handsome, clever and rich' young heroine Emma Woodhouse, whose attitude to marriage for herself is influenced by her father's dislike of it. She doesn't want anyone interfering with her position as 'queen bee' in Highbury. However, she has several character flaws, not least her deluded belief in her own powers of matchmaking, which leads to all kinds of romantic problems, for others particularly. Eventually, when her own happiness is threatened, she realises that interfering in the lives of others can have harmful consequences.

Her eventual understanding that the man she has always relied upon to point out her mistakes – the only person who can, in fact – George Knightley, is the man she loves, which is revealed after an extraordinary picnic at Box Hill. His reproof to her, after she insults a woman much lower than her in station, stings. She has never before felt "so agitated, so mortified, [so] grieved" and she cries all the way home.

'The person, be it gentleman or lady, who has not pleasure in a good novel, must be intolerably stupid.'

HENRY TILNEY, NORTHANGER ABBEY

Northanger Abbey is often a book neglected or ignored by fans of the 'great' works. Published six months after the author's death in 1817, *Northanger Abbey* is a short book containing some of Jane Austen's wittiest quotes. In fact, the 'hero', Henry Tilney, has been compared in character to Jane herself.

Setting out to satirise the 18th-century reader's love of the Gothic novel, such as those written by Ann Radcliffe, *Northanger Abbey* is a clever defence of the art of novel writing. This reflected the Austen family's pleasure in reading fiction, inspired by the Revd. George Austen's library.

The story follows seventeen-year-old Catherine Morland, a contented daughter of a country clergyman, who is taken by neighbours on holiday to Bath for the season. Catherine is not especially clever or witty and lives her life through the lens of an avid reader of the gothic novel. Northanger Abbey is the story of her adventures in a city Austen knew well and she places Catherine, who at first takes everyone on trust and views them as figures in the fiction she reads, at the mercy of a society she enters with a simple naivety. She learns through a growing awareness of the importance of society's expectations. She encounters a problematic friendship, unexpected romance and the politics of social ambition. There are witty exchanges on the subjects of fashion, of reading and of taste, and the book can be seen as a clever exploration of the desire to experience the terror of the gothic.

'All the privilege I claim for my own sex (it is not a very enviable one: you need not covet it), is that of loving longest, when existence or when hope is gone!'

ANNE ELLIOT, PERSUASION

Persuasion has been called 'one of the most tender love stories ever written' by the Jane Austen Society, and it is certainly her most mature, in terms of style, subject and heroine. It was published posthumously with *Northanger Abbey*, its name changed from *The Elliots*, Jane's title when she completed it in 1816, just a year before she died. It is frequently referred to as 'autumnal', a season which is described with poetic positivity in the novel itself, but which more reflects its maturity and sober tone. Jane examines issues of social class, of how society was changing to offer greater social mobility and how the interference of foolish friends and relations creates dilemmas for those concerned with duty and deference. Ultimately, we experience second chances, between characters who have learned with difficulty the importance of deep feelings and the value of true love.

Eight years before the book begins, Anne Elliot, had been persuaded, by her snobbish father and circle of friends, to refuse an offer of marriage from relatively lowly Captain Frederick Wentworth who by the time *Persuasion* opens is now a wealthy naval officer, with rank and respect that sees him fit for any society. Still hurt by Anne's refusal, which she deeply regrets, the novel focuses on the recognition of their continuing love for one another, culminating in perhaps the most romantic of all Jane Austen's love scenes.

Persuasion is a book many read after the giddy delights of *Pride and Prejudice* and *Emma*, wondering whether as Jane grew older she identified more closely with Anne Elliott than any other female character she created.

'The sea air and sea bathing together were nearly infallible, one or the other of them being a match for every disorder of the stomach, the lungs or the blood. They were anti-spasmodic, anti-pulmonary, anti-septic, anti-billious and anti-rheumatic.'

NARRATOR, SANDITON

Sanditon Although also adapted for the screen, readers and audiences have always had to use their powers of imagination to the full when reading the novel Jane had started work on just before her last illness prevented any further writing.

It is an intriguing first few chapters – written as *The Brothers* – which examine, primarily, the contrast between the old and new orders in society, and how money (obtained through inheritance or entrepreneurship) affected leisure and health. In the world of 'fan fiction' Sanditon is a favourite for re-imagination and offers opportunities, with a wonderful cast of characters, including the seaside resort of 'Sanditon' itself, for romance, humour and intrigue.

Her Most Famous Characters

'I hope I never ridicule what is wise or good. Follies and nonsense, whims and inconsistencies do divert me, I own, and I laugh at them whenever I can.'

ELIZABETH BENNET, PRIDE AND PREJUDICE

So says Elizabeth Bennet in *Pride and Prejudice*. As her own favourite character, it can be argued that Elizabeth says those things Jane Austen herself might say in similar situations. But the truth is not so simple. The skill of Jane Austen is to fashion characters, both good and bad, likeable and less so, that seem fully formed on the page and able to represent the themes of her stories. Here are some of the best-known.

'I cannot make speeches, Emma... If I loved you less, I might be able to talk about it more. But you know what I am. You hear nothing but truth from me. I have blamed you, and lectured you, and you have borne it as no other woman in England would have borne it.'

GEORGE KNIGHTLEY

Mr George Knightley is the lead male character in Jane Austen's novel *Emma*, published in late 1815. Before she started the novel, Austen wrote, "I am going to take a heroine whom no one but myself will much like." As a trusted friend of the family for many years, Emma's brother-in-law, George Knightley, is the perfect character to highlight Emma's faults. He is the epitome of the English gentleman, coming from a good family and managing his wealthy estate with integrity. He is always charitable, fair and generous with his time and money.

Devoted to Emma and the development of her character, he openly criticises her when he sees her behaving badly. By the end of the book, after Emma has spent months matchmaking amongst her friends with disastrous consequences, Emma realises her true feelings for this most important of men and happiness is restored.

'I lay it down as a general rule, Harriet, that if a woman doubts as to whether she should accept a man or not, she certainly ought to refuse him.'

EMMA WOODHOUSE

Emma Woodhouse Despite Jane Austen's bleak character description, many people love Emma as the "handsome, clever, and rich" girl with "a comfortable home and happy disposition" as first described by the narrator. Emma lives a life that reinforces all the good things she thinks about herself and those around her at Hartfield and in the village of Highbury.

Twenty-one years old, with a doting father and devoted friend, Emma can make her way through society with time to learn her lessons and seek to make amends. By creating this pretty, intelligent (she has sufficient self-awareness to recognise that although a talented musician, there are others better than herself), but spoiled and privileged girl, Jane Austen can satirise the Georgian obsession with social status and respectability. She is a proto-feminist in some ways, as she seeks to create marital happiness for others without thinking it necessary for her own, but she makes error after error, blindly, for a good part of the book and strains our patience with her. Luckily for her, she has George Knightly as her guardian angel and even when she can't sense his positive influence, the reader can.

'You are mistaken, Mr Darcy, if you suppose that the mode of your declaration affected me in any other way, than as it spared me the concern which I might have felt in refusing you, had you behaved in a more gentlemanlike manner.'

ELIZABETH BENNET

Elizabeth Bennet 'I must confess that I think her as delightful a character as ever appeared in print, and how I shall be able to tolerate those who do not like her at least, I do not know.' Jane Austen to her sister Cassandra 29 January 1813.

As the heroine of *Pride and Prejudice*, Elizabeth Bennet is a favourite Austen character, much beloved by the author herself. In her early twenties she is the second daughter of five. 'Lizzy' is depicted as a beautiful young woman, with intelligence, spirit and wit. She might be young, but she is intelligent and an excellent judge of people (other than Wickham and Darcy), has a degree of self-awareness and, eventually, capacity for admitting that she was wrong. We are always encouraged to look on her as a sympathetic character and are rooting for her happiness, even as we watch her reject the hero and side with the rogue, if only for part of the story. Her willingness to speak her mind, her wit and confidence and her quick reposts, force Darcy to look at his behaviour. Whatever future they have together, in the book it seems it will be of equals, despite the differences in their status and wealth.

'As a child I was taught what was right, but I was not taught to correct my temper. I was given good principles, but left to follow them in pride and conceit.'
DARCY

Fitzwilliam Darcy Hero, villain, rake, or rogue? In fact Fitzwilliam Darcy is none of these – like Elizabeth he has faults, but Jane Austen created a complex character in Darcy, one she gradually unveils as *Pride and Prejudice* progresses. Unlike Wickham or Willoughby, he has none of the rake about him. Neither is he a villain, but he is proud and disagreeable to a new acquaintance, and class conscious to the point of rudeness. His upbringing and immense wealth have given him a sense of overwhelming superiority. Unlike Elizabeth, he is not a character we like at once, or root for, despite his tall and handsome appearance. His initial proposal to Elizabeth is both socially awkward and deeply insulting.

Ultimately, Darcy quietly redeems himself, either through the eyes of his adoring sister and the staff at Pemberley or through his actions in saving Elizabeth's sister Lydia (and thus her whole family) from social ruin. Elizabeth's gradual realisation of his worth and her love is set alongside his constancy – her refusal of his first proposal serves to reflect back at him his behaviour, pride and arrogance and is a catalyst for change.

There is much discussion about whether Darcy is simply 'socially awkward' and shy. Film adaptations might have suggested this, but in the book, Jane Austen is clear – his pride and Elizabeth's initial refusal to believe any good of him are key to the satisfying ending.

'I am afraid,' replied Elinor, 'that the pleasantness of an employment does not always evince its propriety.'

ELINOR.

Elinor Dashwood Elinor is the 'Sense' to her younger sister Marianne's 'Sensibility' in the title of Jane Austen's first completed novel. The eldest daughter of Mr and Mrs Henry Dashwood, at points in the book it is easy to forget she is just nineteen years old, so much support does she give her mother and sister. She is attractive with a 'pretty figure', but contrasts with lively Marianne, and so appears to be more upright and reserved. She might be the model of propriety, but she is devoted to her more spontaneous sister and affectionate to others, putting their needs above her own.

In all things, especially love, Elinor is more cautious and keeps her self-control even when she thinks the man she loves, Edward Ferrars, has married someone else. She is the heroine of the novel, but some readers find her repressed emotions and rational descriptions of people and things frustrating. At the end of the novel, she has found the happiness her goodness and patience deserves, and we realise that under all the stoic refusal to break down under her disappointments she is as emotional and eager to love as Marianne.

'Marianne's abilities were, in many respects, quite equal to Elinor's. She was sensible and clever; but eager in everything: her sorrows, her joys, could have no moderation. She was generous, amiable, interesting: she was everything but prudent.'

Marianne Dashwood Marianne represents 'Sensibility' or feeling and emotion, and although she has a lot in common with the sentimental heroines of novels of the period, she is also used by Jane Austen as a balance and reflection of her elder sister Elinor's character. By the end of the book, Jane Austen has established that between the two sisters lies the best balance of 'sense and sensibility'.

At the beginning of the book, Marianne is only just over sixteen. With a head full of romance and powerful feelings, she finds it astonishing that her sister Elinor can be attracted to someone as reserved as Edward Ferrars, whom she believes has 'something wanting'. Her passions and her 'whole heart' settle on the feckless John Willoughby, who abandons her to marry for money. Her heart is broken and her desolation makes her desperately ill. Elinor nurses her back to health, and a recognition that the true love of a man who has always adored her – Colonel Brandon – can be as worthy of her love.

'We have all a better guide in ourselves, if we would attend to it, than any other person can be.'

FANNY.

Fanny Price As the lead character in *Mansfield Park*, Fanny Price is a different Austen heroine – quiet, meek, morally upright and convinced, in her lowly status, that she "can never be important to anyone." She is small in stature and perhaps in personality. If a reader was expecting the sparkling wit of previous female characters, they would be let down.

However, Jane Austen does not allow her characters to lack purpose. Fanny is a listener, with a generosity of spirit that contrasts with her neighbours

Henry and Mary Crawford, neither of whom achieves the happy ending we hope for Fanny and Edmund, her cousin and the love of her life. She is observant and fearless in her determination not to submit to the will of fearsome men with their own motives.

Interestingly, at the time of the novel, the marriage of Fanny to Edmund would have been legal, but not encouraged, and throughout the novel they appear to consider themselves more like brother and sister. One of Jane Austen's brothers, Henry, married their first cousin Eliza and perhaps Fanny's happiness was to reflect and support their happiness.

'If I was wrong in yielding to persuasion once, remember that it was persuasion exerted on the side of safety, not of risk.'

ANNE.

Anne Elliot Anne is the middle daughter of the widowed Sir Walter Elliot in *Persuasion*, published posthumously in 1817. She has to deal with an extravagant and vain father, a selfish elder sister and a younger one obsessed with her health, and herself. Both sisters are married and at 27, Anne is considered a spinster.

An intelligent, independent young woman, surrounded by those who cannot appreciate her wit and thoughtfulness, she is somewhat lonely. She deeply regrets having refused Frederick Wentworth, now a respected and wealthy naval captain, eight years previously, and has become thin, believing her face is a 'ruin' and unattractive to Wentworth when he reappears in her life. Jane Austen, as the narrator, describes her as having lost her youthful bloom, but in letters the author recognised her character's goodness, which marks her out as many readers favourite heroine.

Anne remains loyal to her difficult family and even believes she made the right decision in initially refusing Wentworth. She is self-aware and reflective, and despite being more mature and experienced than Jane Austen's other heroines, she has the capacity for growth. By the end of the novel, she has kept her integrity whilst still achieving the happiness she deserves with the man she has always loved. Interestingly, he is the only self-made man Jane Austen gives her heroines to, marking perhaps the social shift to the growing wealthy middle classes.

Henry: 'I consider a country-dance as an emblem of marriage. Fidelity and complaisance are the principal duties of both; and those men who do not choose to dance or marry themselves, have no business with the partners or wives of their neighbours.'

Catherine: 'But they are such very different things! –'

Henry: '– That you think they cannot be compared together.'

Catherine: 'To be sure not. People that marry can never part, but must go and keep house together. People that dance only stand opposite each other in a long room for half an hour.'

Catherine Morland and Henry Tilney in *Northanger Abbey* are a couple who provide the most fun and the warmest hearts in the book.

At the start of the novel, Catherine is a naïve seventeen-year-old, who finds herself thrust into the social whirl of the Bath season. Largely self-educated by the pages of gothic novels and poetry books, she takes people at face value and refuses to think the worst of them until there is no alternative. Her loyalty is a great virtue, but at times it is misused. She thinks the manipulative Isabella Thorp is a great friend, but even when misused, only abandons her for the love of her family. As the book progresses, and her true friendship with and love for siblings Henry and Eleanor Tilney develops, it is clear Catherine is learning from her errors and moderating her enthusiasm for all things Romantic.

Henry Tilney is not the usual masterful hero of Jane Austen's novels, but he is one of the easiest to love. "He seemed to be about four or five and twenty, was rather tall, had a pleasing countenance, a very intelligent and lively eye, and, if not quite handsome, was very near it." Jane Austen describes Henry in charming terms and that charm is clear from his actions and demeanour throughout the book. He is well-read, not snooty about novels, and can converse with women on the subject of muslin. Always well-mannered, he falls in love with Catherine and would marry her despite her lack of wealth. Conversations between them are witty and fun and Jane Austen's own love of reading is woven through the text, often in Henry's words.

In spite of the initial success of her novels, it didn't take long for them to go out of favour. The Victorians regarded the lack of respect for clergymen as irreverent. Mr Collins's obsequiousness to Lady Caroline de Burgh was satirical, but to a Victorian it was quite appropriate, and genteel. Genteel was something her heroines were not, either. The behaviour of young women later in the 19th century was expected to be less, not more independent and Elizabeth Bennet, for example, was a terrible literary example for young women.

However, towards the end of the 19th century, and with the publication of her nephew's biography, that interest in her was rekindled. By the First World War, and at the centenary of her death in 1917, she was the epitome of Englishness, creating a world worth fighting for; an idyllic rural existence that took young men like poet Siegfried Sassoon out of the trenches. Her books – perhaps even prescribed to damaged young soldiers with shell shock – were the most widely read novels during the war.

By this time, Jane Austen had a wide readership, and was gaining respect from a literary community who had previously viewed novels of the Georgian period as somewhat sentimental, unrealistic and romantic. In 1917, *The Graphic* paper wrote:

'In direct contrast to those forgotten stories of exaggerated sentiment or pseudo-romance which were so popular in Jane Austen's days, her novels hold the mirror faithfully to the rural English life of the time. Therein is their lasting charm…'

Her popularity extended to the literary community. In her 1925 essay on Jane Austen, Virginia Woolf described her as "the most perfect artist among women."

The war and the inter-war period encouraged escape. Golden Age crime writers gave readers the opportunity to leave behind hard lives and solve murders from their sofas. Agatha Christie is said to have admired Jane Austen, and new editions were being brought out to satisfy the general demand. *The Aberdeen Press and Journal*, on 18th October, 1926, said:

'Partially because these are days of flurry and rush many prefer for their leisure reading hours literature that is dignified, placid, and unhurried... there is a perennial charm too in her exquisite cameo style and the delicate, satiric twist of her character portraits... while Mr R. W. Chapman brought out a new edition in five volumes in 1923, the Oxford University Press now think it opportune to send out a reissue.'

The novels have always been well-suited for adaptation and re-imagination. In 1936, Mrs Helen Jerome starred in a stage adaptation of *Pride and Prejudice* and since then, on big and small screen, readers of her work and new admirers enjoyed Colin Firth and Jennifer Ehle as Darcy and Elizabeth, Emma Thompson and Kate Winslet as Elinor and Marianne and Gwynneth Paltrow as Emma, films later remade with stars such as Keira Knightley and Kate Beckinsale. Anne Hathaway has played Jane herself and A list stars seem to consider a part in an adaptation as a privilege.

The novels are admired by general readers and academics alike and have been translated into over 30 languages.

MODERN INTERPRETATIONS

Jane Austen and her work have also provided inspiration for many other successful novels. Helen Fielding, the author of *Bridget Jones's Diary*, freely admits she took the plot from *Pride and Prejudice* and, for recent audiences, the *Bridgerton* series of books, now filmed for streaming services, has rekindled a love for the fashions and passions of the Georgian era. The great British crime novelist P. D. James wrote a historical mystery, *Death Comes to Pemberley*, which continued the story of *Pride and Prejudice*, adding the murder and criminal trial of characters from the original novel. There are now cosy crime novels where Jane Austen solves murders, or where the detectives are the children of Elizabeth and Darcy. There are romantic reworkings of the stories, set in different ages and different cultures. *Bride and Prejudice,* from 2004, reworked the story of Darcy and Elizabeth and took it to India looking, with laughter, at the modern pressures on four daughters in one Indian family. The themes in *Pride and Prejudice* have been particularly

successful at inspiring contemporary authors to reimagine the romance, and there is the now classic *Pride and Prejudice and Zombies* by Seth Grahame-Smith, a splicing together of classic and zombie literature.

Grahame-Smith's book was made into a film in 2016, to mixed reviews. In other films, the 1995 film *Clueless*, based on *Emma* and updated to an American high school, successfully recreates the 'little rich girl matchmaker' themes of the novel and a musical version is coming to the stage.

In 2007, *Becoming Jane* was released, a fictionalised account of Jane's romantic life, focused on Tom Lefroy but suggesting that there were many other suitors in her life. Perhaps it is difficult to believe that someone so acutely aware of the manners and morals of Georgian relationships should not have found a life partner herself.

Author Kate Mosse believes that Agatha Christie's Miss Marple might not have been created had Christie not been an Austen enthusiast. The unmarried woman, living without the stresses of domestic life, can be an observer, commenting with wit on the weaknesses of others.

At the time of Jane Austen's death in 1817, there existed no 'Janeites', no recognition of her literary talents as an author, aside from those attributed to 'a Lady'. The reasons we often turn to Jane Austen's novels, whether in print or on film, during times of stress and for relaxation, are her humour and sharp wit, her skill in satire, and as *The Graphic* emphasised in 1917:

'… that sweetness of disposition to which all her relatives and friends bore unanimous testimony. Hence when death claimed her at too-early age it is not surprising her relatives estimated their greatest loss in the terms of her character than that in the deprivation of her genius.'

Chronology

JANE'S LIFE		LITERARY & GLOBAL EVENTS
Revd Austen takes the living of Steventon	1764	
James Austen, Jane's brother born	1765	
Brother Edward Austen born	1766	
	1770	Wordsworth born
Henry born	1771	
	1772	Coleridge born
Cassandra, Jane's older sister, born	1773	
Francis born	1774	
Jane Austen born 16th December	1775	
	1776	Declaration of American Independence
Charles, Jane's youngest brother, born	1780	
Cassandra and Jane sent to boarding school in Oxford, later moving to Southampton where both very ill. Jane almost dies of typhus	1783	End of the American War of Independence Pitt the Younger becomes Prime Minister of Britain

1785
Study in Reading before returning to Steventon
1787
Begins writing, including Lady Susan and Love and Friendship
1788
George Gordon Byron born
George III temporarily insane
1789
French Revolution begins
1792
Mary Wollstonecraft Vindications of the Rights of Women
Percy Bysshe Shelley born
1793
Execution of Louis XIV
1794
1795
Writes Elinor and Marianne, later revising and naming it Sense and Sensibility
John Keats born
Prince of Wales (later Regent) marries Caroline of Brunswick
1796
Writes First Impressions, later renaming it Pride and Prejudice
Bonaparte invades Italy and threatens England
1797
George Austen offers First Impressions to a publisher but it is turned down
Mary Wollstonecraft Godwin (later Mary Shelley) born
1798
Jane writes Susan, later to become Northanger Abbey
Lyrical Ballads published by Wordsworth and Coleridge
1801
George Austen retires from the Steventon living. Family to Bath

Jane Austen's life	Year	World events
Jane accepts, then rejects a marriage proposal	1802	
Susan revised and sold to Crosby. Jane receives £10	1803	Renewal of war with France
Revd Austen, Jane's father, dies.	1805	Battle of Trafalgar and victory for Nelson
Jane and Cassandra move to Southampton with their mother	1806	Britain abolishes the slave trade
Jane and Cassandra and Mrs Austen to Chawton in Hampshire. *Susan* returned by publisher	1809	Wordsworth publishes *Guide to the Lakes* George III declared insane
Revises *Sense and Sensibility* and pays for publication by T Egerton of Whitehall	1810	Prince of Wales made Regent Luddite attacks begin
Sense and Sensibility published, written by 'A Lady'	1811	John Keats born Prince of Wales (later Regent) marries Caroline of Brunswick
Pride and Prejudice finished. Jane sells manuscript for £110	1812	Robert Browning born Charles Dickens born Two-year war with USA begins British Prime Minister, Perceval, is assassinated.
Publication of *Pride and Prejudice* *Sense and Sensibility* goes into a second edition Jane completes *Mansfield Park*	1813	

1814

Mansfield Park published

Napoleon abdicates

Leigh Hunt convicted of seditious libel

1815

Emma completed and published. *Persuasion* (first titled *The Elliots*) begun.

Napoleon escapes from Elba

Battle of Waterloo

1816

Persuasion completed in July.

First signs of the serious illness that quickly disables Jane

1817

Jane and Cassandra move to Winchester for Jane's health.

Sanditon begun (first titled '*The Brothers*') but just 12 chapters completed.

Jane Austen dies on 18 July, aged 41.

Burial at Winchester Cathedral 24th July

Habeus Corpus suspended

Keats *Poems* published

1818

Persuasion and *Northanger Abbey* published posthumously. For the first time Jane's name appears as author.

Mary Shelley publishes *Frankenstein*

1819

The Peterloo Massacre

1869

In December, *A Memoir of Jane Austen*, is published. The first biography, it is written by her nephew James Edward Austen-Leigh.

1925

Sanditon published under the title *A Fragment of a Novel*

Index

Sources

Bibliography

Jane Austen Selected Letters Ed. R.W. Chapman OUP1955

Jane Austen and her World Marghanita Laski Thames & Hudson 1969

A Portrait of Jane Austen – David Cecil Constable 1978

Jane Austen Carol Shields Orion 2001

Jane Austen A Life Claire Tomalin Penguin 2012

Eavesdropping on Jane Austen's England Roy & Lesley Adkins 2013

Jane Austen at Home Lucy Worsley Hodder 2017

Jane Austen in Sydney Gardens (Leaflet) Diana White & the Sydney Gardens Project

Acknowledgements

I would like to acknowledge the contribution of all the Janeites and Austenites out there who have studied, clarified and promoted the works of Jane Austen. To some, she feels like a friend, to others, an object of study and interpretation, and I have found both to be equally important when examining biographies, searching for appropriate quotes and establishing references.

My thanks to The London Library for its continued support of my writing. and for the long loans, often sent by post, of wonderful books on Jane in their stores. I am also grateful to the customers of Framlingham Bookshop, where I am a bookseller. Jane Austen fans amongst them have been cheering me on as they see me sitting behind the counter adding to the word count in quiet moments.

Thanks to my editor, Tania Ahsan, for offering me this opportunity to highlight the wit, wisdom and 21st-century relevance of such a remarkable woman, and to Jen Boyle, who gave me my first publishing deal all those years ago and suggested I take this project on.

And to my lovely family, who had to listen to me going 'Oooo listen to this one!' more than 52 times in the development of the cards. Jane Austen was a wise woman. We can do worse than wonder *What Would Jane Do?*